The Colorado : River of Mystery

The COLORADO:

RIVER OF MYSTERY

By Mary and Conrad Buff

THE WARD RITCHIE PRESS : LOS ANGELES

To Major John Wesley Powell
Selfless Explorer of the Colorado River

COPYRIGHT © 1968 BY MARY MARSH BUFF AND CONRAD BUFF
LIBRARY OF CONGRESS CARD NUMBER 68-30700
DESIGNED BY JOSEPH SIMON
LITHOGRAPHED IN THE UNITED STATES OF AMERICA
BY ANDERSON, RITCHIE & SIMON

Table of Contents

v

1. The River of Mystery

Other rivers of America—the Hudson, the Potomac, the Mississippi—are "water roads," from whose mouths explorers entered the land. Settlers followed, building log houses along the streams. Thus civilization spread up the river valleys.

But the Colorado River is different. It fights man every inch of his way, as he travels either upstream or down, and has done this for thousands and thousands of years.

Where it flows into the ocean at the Gulf of California, a huge tidal wave, or "bore," rushes upstream for over thirty-five miles at times, battling the downcoming current. In this war of the waves, boats going up or coming down the river were often wrecked. Near its mouth lie sunken rocks, sand bars, and snags unseen beneath the red waters. Thus exploration of the land from the mouth of the Colorado River has never been successful, as in other rivers of America.

Nor has it been safe to descend the stream. In its middle course, it flows between sheer cliffs, over a mile high. Between these walls, the Colorado roars and booms in countless cataracts, "white water," and whirlpools.

1

So it is easy to understand why this great desert stream has been called the River of Mystery for many hundreds of years.

Terrifying stories were told about it even before the Spaniards entered the land. The Indians, seated around their evening fires, warned each other of this fearsome river, firmly believing the entire stream plunged into a great underground hole, never again returning to the light. They claimed they heard the roar of buried waters from the rim above.

Later, white men feared the Colorado, too. The Spaniards were awed by it. The beaver hunters of the 1800's hated it and enlarged upon the stories they heard from the Indians. Spinners of yarns told of fellow trappers who were upset in the rapids of the stream and had died of starvation, unable to climb out of the abyss.

Soldiers followed the trappers. In lonely frontier posts, before the Civil War, army men entertained each other with legends of the River of Mystery.

There were falls in this stream, they claimed, greater than any man had ever seen. The Plateau on the rim was dangerous also, for it was waterless. Men had died of thirst, staring down into the muddy Colorado from cliffs too steep to descend. Thirst-crazed sheep had plunged over the high ledges when breezes from the river brought them the smell of water.

As these stories passed from mouth to mouth, they grew more fantastic. Although many of them were false, all of them were built upon the basic fact that the Colorado was unknown. No man could deny these tales, for no one knew the real truth.

At that time, no living being had gone through the chasms

of the great river and returned to tell others what he had seen. Until Major John Wesley Powell in 1869 embarked upon his great adventure—the geographical and geological survey of this body of water—the Colorado was the River of Mystery, as it had been for over three hundred years.

CLOUDBURSTS AND CANYONS

In the far West of our land lies the Plateau country, almost five hundred miles wide. It is separated from the Mississippi Valley by the snow-capped Rocky Mountains and from the cool Pacific Ocean by the saw-toothed Sierras.

Like a great tabletop, it dips gently from north to south. In Wyoming, it is a mile above the ocean. At the border of Mexico, eight hundred miles away, it reaches sea level.

On Plateau land, summer days are blistering hot; yet summer nights, under velvety skies, are cool.

Compared with other lands, the Plateau country is naked. Its bony skeleton juts up in flat-topped hills and sharp, needle-like peaks. Stunted piñon, sagebrush, and dwarf oak barely cover its rocky ribs; dew never falls, and rains come seldom.

In some places it is so dry that the mark of a wagon wheel may be found years after the wagon has creaked away. An explorer, new to the starved country, struggles through sand as dry as ashes. He may die of thirst if he is not desert-wise. The few springs of the Plateau are slyly hidden. The gullies of deep desert rivers are bone-dry, except during summer storms.

On the distant skyline, a phantom lake shimmers. The wan-

4

derer longs to drink its waters, but the lake retreats as he labors through the sand. He will never reach that lake. It does not exist. He has seen a mirage which fools even those who know the desert well.

Strange plants spread their weather-beaten arms, a store of water against the drought hidden in their pulpy leaves. They are cacti. If they did not protect their treasure of water with countless stinging needles, thirsty animals would steal that water.

The spring flowers of these bristling veterans are surprising. They teem with blossoms—red, yellow, white—delicate and charming, like fairy daughters of an ugly ogre.

Animals are rarer than plants. Unless Nature has fitted them to live in a dry and cruel country, they seek pleasanter places. Except for lizards, that constantly dart about his feet, the wanderer may see nothing but a horned toad, a tarantula, or a scorpion.

In a faultless sky he may watch an eagle, searching the gray world below for his enemy, the rattlesnake. A buzzard or vulture may circle low around a sick coyote or wounded jackrabbit, waiting for the animal to die.

As the wanderer struggles over a featureless land, he may suddenly come upon a great crack in the earth. It is so narrow, he can throw a rock across it. His knees may tremble, as he peers down into a chasm perhaps a thousand feet deep, where a single green willow proves the presence of water.

This is the channel of a desert river, dry most of the year but, in the stormy season, violent with muddy, red water.

The Plateau land is chiseled with such deep chasms. How are they made?

The brief rains fall in midsummer. They come without warning.

A black, billowy cloud collects from nowhere. It is over-charged with moisture. A cold wind strikes it; bfff—it explodes as suddenly as a balloon pricked with a pin. Down, down upon the dry earth plunges a deluge of rain. This is a cloudburst.

The water falls so fast, it has no time to soak into a thirsty earth but runs off, as from the roof of a house. Finding the nearest slope, the water carves a little gully. Rushing downward, it grabs sand and pebbles as it hurries on.

Armed with biting sand, the torrent scours the gully deeper. When it joins another such ravine, a canyon begins. Finally it flows into the deepest canyon of the Plateau land— the Colorado River.

By the time the brown turmoil has reached the greatest river of the West, the place where the cloudburst fell may be entirely dry; the skies clear, though but a half hour may have passed.

But the cloudburst has done its work well. It has carved a pathway in the dry land which will be cut deeper the next time a storm comes. So, as the years pass, the canyon will become ever deeper.

In this way, the great, deep gorges of the entire Colorado River system were formed.

*   *   *

But there are still other reasons for the immense depths of canyon rivers, especially of the Colorado River.

Geologists, who read the history of the world's creation by studying its rocks, say the Plateau land once lay at the bottom of a great sea. Forces beneath the earth, about which we know little, pushed the land up from this ocean.

As time passed, the entire Plateau land sank back again into the salty ocean waters.

Thousands and thousands of years passed. Sometimes the Plateau land was above the sea, sometimes under the sea.

In recent geologic times, the underneath-land forces once more lifted the country above the ocean. It remained there and slowly kept on rising. *Then*, we believe, the entire Colorado River system was first laid down.

The Colorado River, once formed, was a stubborn and strong-willed river. As the land slowly rose, the river rose too, unchanged. They rested together, a mile or more above the ocean.

If the young river had relied upon the few rains that fell over the dry plateau, it would soon have died. But it was fed constantly by snow waters from the Rocky Mountains at its source.

At first these waters were clear. But the river was over a mile above the sea, so its velocity as it flowed was great. The dry land had little plant life to hold it together, and it began to carry more sand, pebbles, even boulders with it, as it hurried down to the sea.

Sand and pebbles are sharp grinding tools in the claws of a swift stream. With such chisels a river cuts a deep channel quickly. This cutting-down of a stream bed is called *corrosion*.

As the years went by, the energetic Colorado ate deep and still deeper into the wastelands it drained, while the Plateau land changed slowly. The tools that change a land are rains, snows, frosts, and winds. This is called *erosion*.

As corrosion went on rapidly in the river, erosion proceeded much more slowly on the land. Thus the bed of the river was always deeper than the land.

This is why the Plateau remained higher than the river. This is how the deep chasms of the Colorado River were finally carved down to the original rock of which the earth was formed.

2. From Glacier to Sea

Among the many tributaries of the Colorado River only three, the Green, Upper Colorado and San Juan, flow constantly, being fed from melting snows of the Rockies.

Other tributaries drain the Plateau, but they are "wet weather" streams and flow only in times of storm.

Of these, the Little Colorado is the most typical. One day sluggish pools of brown water may lie in its thirty-five hundred foot canyon. The next day it may be a raging torrent caused by rain from a distant cloudburst on the desert.

But if the Colorado relied upon such fickle tributaries it would soon die. Melting snows alone keep the giant river of the West alive.

GREEN RIVER

The Green is the more interesting of the two main tributaries of the Colorado. Its canyons are strangely beautiful. Major Powell descended this tributary in 1869 to reach the Colorado. Many of the explorers that followed him have taken the same route. When Powell made his first voyage he named each chasm as he passed through it. His fine feeling for the varied character of each has made those names used to this day.

INFANCY

On the western slope of the Wind River Mountains in Wyoming, Fremont Peak pushes its icy cap into the sky. Here is born Green River, of glaciers and Alpine lakes, where deer abound and fawns hide under the ferns.

The young stream romps down through the sweet-smelling forests. At the foot of the mountains it is already a wide river.

Spruce and pine vanish as cacti, piñon, and the ever-present sagebrush appear. In the sandy river bottoms sprawl willow and cottonwood, lovers of moisture.

A few miles south of where the Union Pacific Railroad crosses the river, the first of the typical canyons begins—Flaming Gorge—followed by smaller gorges.

Then, turning east, the river finds the Uinta Mountains blocking its way. Now energetic, strong, and youthful, it cuts through the very heart of these granite mountains, its teeth sharpened by sand it has gathered from the desert wastes. It carves its first great canyon, the Canyon of Lodore.

Lodore has an evil history. Major Powell, in his first exploration of the Colorado system, lost a boat in its wild rapids. Trappers and explorers have drowned in the foaming waters that continue for about twenty miles. But then the Green settles

down and enters the lonely, weary stretch in Utah known as Desolation Canyon.

For one hundred and thirty-five miles the river, slowly growing redder and redder with sand, hastens on, harried by dust storms. Cliffs of soft red sandstone are riddled with ancient Indian cave dwellings. From the rim the "bad lands" stretch east and west, windswept and pockmarked—a desolate place indeed.

Soon the San Rafael River joins the Green, and for a few miles the arid desert gives birth to the green fields of Gunnison's Crossing. But soon these are no more. Once again the Green, like a lazy snake asleep in the sun, winds through Labyrinth Canyon, doubling back upon itself in great, sinuous oxbows that oftentimes seem to meet as they wind through labyrinths of colored gorges.

Cliff dwellings dot the walls; old irrigation ditches tell the history of the vanished red man. Wild horses come down to drink in the river. Sure-footed mountain sheep skim the cliffs. On the rim for miles stretches the "Land of Standing Rocks," as the Indians called that vast wilderness.

Then a tributary joins the Green from the northeast. It is as large as the Green. It is the upper Colorado, called the Grand until 1921. This twin to the Green rises in snow mountains west of Long's Peak in Colorado. Its course is, like the Green, through an arid land. Within the last few years scientists have found it carries slightly more water than its brother the Green river, and this is why its name was changed to the Colorado.

The great tributaries unite. Now the childhood of the river is over.

For a few miles the rivers wrestle like playful bear cubs, trying to overcome each other. Huge waves are thrown in the air
from their struggle. No one is the victor as they mingle to work
together cutting deep into Cataract Canyon between hard rocks,
the walls rising three thousand feet in places.

In the two hundred miles to Lee's Ferry, the Colorado now
presents a most varied picture. In the first forty miles through
Cataract Canyon, it moans and claws at the rocks, impetuous,
boisterous, the graveyard of explorers—as dangerous a river as
exists.

But when the Fremont River joins the Colorado from the
west, the walls lower, and for one hundred and fifty miles the
Colorado flows through Glen Canyon, the most charming canyon of all, like peace after war, light after dark.

Natural bridges and kingly arches are everywhere in the soft
red sandstone, and narrow side canyons where mosses and ferns
hide. Cliff dwellings and Indian picture-carvings continue, tell-
ing of the deeds and hopes of red hunters.

From the rim above in the distance lies the dark blue dome of
Navajo Mountain, sacred to the Indians, and six miles from the
river, famous Rainbow Bridge.

Soon the Crossing of the Fathers is reached. Here Father
Escalante crossed in 1776, and later the Ute Indians swam their
horses over the stream to harry Mormons who lived to the Westward.

When Paria Creek joins the Colorado at Lee's Ferry, now

under the waters of Lake Powell, the youth of the river is over. Manhood lies ahead.

MANHOOD

Lee's Ferry is an historical place where John D. Lee, a Mormon involved in the murder of immigrants, fled and hid for years. He built a log house, tilled a few acres of bottom land, and from a watchtower on the cliffs kept on the lookout for officers of the law who constantly searched for him.

In 1872 Lee built a ferry, giving the place its name. Here he ferried Mormons across the Colorado, bound for settlements in Utah. He was able to evade the law for years until one day he left the ferry for supplies and was captured and executed.

Now, at Lee's Ferry, government scientists measure the daily flow of the great river. A steel bridge spans the rim at the head of Marble Canyon. This is the only bridge for hundreds of miles by which one can cross the river except for the road over the Glen Canyon Dam. Many miles south automobiles can again cross the Colorado at Hoover Dam.

GRAND CANYON

At Lee's Ferry, land and river are almost on the same level. But only a few miles southwest the eager Colorado dives into the bowels of Marble Canyon. As the land rises and the Little Colorado flows in from the east, the mature river rages in a four thousand foot canyon, cutting into the First Granite Gorge of the Grand Canyon.

In the span of over two hundred miles this river of rivers grinds down two thousand feet—a descent unknown in any other stream—chiseling, cutting, biting into the very rocks of our original globe.

From the South Rim, a mile above the river, one sees the Grand Canyon. It is vast and unworldly, seeming to belong to a strange planet in a solar system not our own. There is nothing on our earth with which to compare it.

The rocky temples, buttes, castle-like cliffs that rise from that silent void are alike yet not alike, just as a melody, repeated by flute, violin, and 'cello, is the same yet not the same.

River and erosion, from sand to wind, have together carved countless rock forms, each one unlike the other. Red sandstone and yellow limestone, of the same hue and thickness, appear in each rocky butte and fortress, like brilliant threads running through a silver tapestry. The color of the Grand Canyon is like the inside of a sea shell, softened by great distances.

The size of this dead world is as far beyond our understanding as the thoughts of an astronomer in his observatory. The dark blue north rim can be seen from the south rim almost fifteen miles away. It is not a grass-covered plain, as it appears, but the great Kaibab Forest, where thousands of deer live among pines and aspens.

The slender ribbon of brown, shining water far below, playing hide and seek in the depths of the Grand Canyon, is not a rivulet but the angry Colorado, four hundred feet wide. Neither are the dark, moving specks on the trail far below insects, but horses and men.

20

On both north and south rims of the river grow pines, spruce, and juniper native to the northern countries. As the trail descends they disappear. The plants of the south spring up among the rocks—the white-belled yucca, the round barrel cactus, the prickly pear, and feathery acacia. In a brief mile from rim to river, plant life changes as widely as from the northern state of Montana to the southern state of Arizona.

Fossils buried in the rocks of the canyon walls tell the story of life emerging from the sea. In the bottom of the gorge, where the first stratified rocks were laid upon the original granite of which the world was made, remnants of the very earliest marine life are imbedded.

Ascending the canyon walls, fossils of later animals are hidden, while on the upper rocks the remains of mammals complete the story of evolution. Nowhere can the student read so clearly as here the story of the world's age, its making and remaking.

OLD AGE

Exhausted by the great effort of carving the Grand Canyon, the river emerges older and weaker. The dizzy descents are over.

When Boulder Dam bars the stream to form Lake Mead a hundred miles long, only a part of the water slips through the barriers, returning to the stream bed much smaller and weaker. The Colorado now flows wearily southward, draining the same desert it has known since youth.

At Parker Dam it loses more of its lifeblood to the aqueduct for teeming and thirsty Los Angeles, and still more at Yuma for the fields of Imperial Valley and the Gila River project. Water is their life essence. There would be no civilization without it.

Now a shrunken old man, the Colorado crosses the International line. In the hot, sticky delta its mind seems to wander as it meanders back and forth in side channels where rattlesnakes coil among cattails and wild burros hide. The tidal bore rushes up from the Gulf. The warrior river has scarcely enough strength to overcome it. And then, almost two thousand miles from its cradle in the snow, this most varied, moody, and glorious river of the West mingles its heavy brown waters with the blue of the gulf sea (called the Sea of Cortez). Gulls watch its death in this lonely place as the Colorado River sinks to its tomb in the great Pacific Ocean.

The official name is now Hoover Dam. It was formerly called Boulder Dam and is still frequently called by that name. The author has used the names interchangeably.

3. Man and the River

THE CLIFF DWELLERS

Indians lived along the River of Mystery centuries before the coming of white men. In some favored places, ledges of hard roof projected toward the river, like overhanging roofs. Beneath these roofs, the cliff dwellers built their stone homes.

High above the stream, these dwellings were reached only by trails from below which the patient Indians cut in solid rock with their primitive stone hammers. No enemy could reach them from above, shielded as they were by the great, overhanging stone ledges.

Through small openings in their stone houses, these peaceful Indians kept watch for warrior enemies who might attack from below. When such foes appeared, the cliff dwellers rolled great

23

rocks down upon them and shot swarms of arrows from the holes of their fortresses. Thus they could keep a host of enemies at bay just as long as corn was stored in their bins and water in their jars.

So for countless years these primitive Indians planted corn and beans along the river bottom and hunted game on the plateau above. Finally they disappeared, we do not know why or how. Some scientists claim they joined the Hopi Indians of Arizona; others believe that they became the ancestors of the Blue Water Indians living still in the Grand Canyon. But now they are gone. Their stone houses crumble slowly away in the lonely red cliffs in many places along the Colorado River.

BUFFALO HUNTERS

Along the headwaters of the River of Mystery once roamed restless Indian hunters—the Crows, Shoshone, Cheyenne, the Snakes, Utes, and Arapaho.

These Indians followed the yearly migrations of countless bison, or buffalo, that gave them all they needed to live—their food, their clothing, their shelter. But the Indians crossed the great river only during hunting expeditions.

Farther south along the Colorado, in the regions east and west of the Grand Canyon, lived the Navajo, Apache, Shewits, Pai Utes, Walpai—hunters, warriors, wanderers.

The Navajo, in particular, feared "Old Age" river, as they called the Colorado. Legends told of their gods who had carved this deep river trail to the Other World, making it the western boundary of their ancient land. Even today, few Navajo Indians cross "Old Age" river without fearing the warning of the gods.

Still farther south, in the delta lands near the mouth of the Colorado River lived the Yumas, the Mojaves, Pimas, and Cocopahs—chiefly farmers. The Colorado was the source of their life. When spring floods had receded, leaving the lowlands carpeted with rich, red mud, the Indians threw their seeds into the slime. The hot southern sun brought their maize and beans to harvest.

Now almost a century has passed since prairie Indians chased vast buffalo herds; since the Navajo and Apache raided peaceful Indian pueblos and pioneer caravans; since the Cocopahs farmed the muddy wastes of the delta lands.

The red man lives no longer his free and restless life. The buffalo have disappeared. Indian tribes are passing away. As they shrink, the stories of their colorful past fade into legends.

But strange to relate, in a hidden, side canyon of the Colorado River, not far from Bright Angel Trail in the Grand Canyon, there still live the Blue Water Indians (Havasupai), unchanged by the modern world beyond their refuge.

BLUE WATER INDIANS

Midway between the pine-clad rim of the Grand Canyon and the muddy Colorado, a mile below, lies the humble village of the Blue Water Indians. An age-old trail, leading down to it, dives from the rim into the abyss. Red men, long dead, carved it from solid rock. One can see the marks of their primitive stone tools.

The dizzy path etches its slow way along the sides of sheer cliffs. Lifeless walls reflect the burning light of the desert sun. The trail descends for miles, then suddenly hundreds of springs ooze forth from the arid, red cliffs.

The rills unite, blue and lovely, dancing down to form Havasu Creek. They are impregnated with carbonate of lime, which gives a rich blue color to Havasu Creek and from which the Indians have taken their name.

Below lies a green valley tucked in between red cliffs, an oasis in the desert. Only a half mile wide, a few miles long, it is sweet with waving corn, peach trees, and emerald patches of alfalfa, more beautiful because of the lifeless desert about it.

Along Havasu Creek are scattered less than fifty conical huts of willow, the village of the Indians, for the tribe is small, less than two hundred.

Below the straggling village, Havasu Creek foams downward in a series of romantic waterfalls. The last and highest of these the Indians call "Mother of Waters." Nearby are abandoned rock dwellings, a crumbling fortress, and food granaries—the former homes of the Blue Water Indians before they moved into willow huts along the river.

It is still twenty miles before the winding, blue creek joins the red Colorado far below, cutting a narrow, crooked chasm that is impossible to ascend.

We do not know when or how these interesting Indians first

26

found the life-giving springs of Havasu Canyon. They themselves claim they once lived along the Little Colorado, tributary of the great Colorado. Probably then they were cliff dwellers.

A little less than two centuries ago, a Spanish friar, Father Garcés, visited them in their present retreat and found them living then much as they do today.

Within recent years, Indians of other tribes visited them, eager to barter for fruit, vegetables, baskets, red ochre, blue indigo, and, above all, for the fine buckskin the women made.

While other Indians made buckskin too, the women of the Blue Water tribe seemed to have a secret. Their buckskin was whiter, stronger, and softer than that of other Indians. It was made from the hides of deer and elk which the hunters killed each fall on the rim of the Grand Canyon.

For this much-prized buckskin, Indians from the distant Rio Grande country crossed the pitiless desert; Hopis from their mesa villages drove sheep down the steep trail or burros loaded with pottery. The Navajo brought colorful blankets to barter.

A Zuni Indian described the canyon home of the Blue Water Indians as follows:

"They are our younger brothers. They live in a land of summer down in a cold country. They sit still in a canyon so deep that a little stone rolled down from the top sounds like thunder ere it strikes the bottom. It is so deep down that only a little while in the middle of the day can one see the sun from below."

These words are still true of these gentle people, whose proudest boast is that they have never killed a white man. Even the gold-crazy prospectors who penetrated their haven in the last century were escorted, unhurt, from the willow village, with the warning never to return.

So live the Blue Water Indians today, much as they have always lived, building their aqueducts, tending their fields. The two trails that lead down to their canyon home are still dangerous for intruders to travel. Some curious ones still do, but isolation has kept the Blue Water Indians largely unchanged.

When the pine trees on the rim are heavy with snow, when winds blow fiercely over the Grand Canyon, the Blue Water Indians "sit still in a canyon so deep that a little stone rolled down from the top sounds like thunder ere it strikes the bottom," just as the Zuni Indians said so many years ago.

SEVEN GOLDEN CITIES

How long primitive man dwelt in the Southwest is not known, for he left few records behind him. Like a tree or a flower, he took from Nature no more than he needed to live. He did not waste or kill for sport. He always knew his children must live in the land after he was gone. He would not waste or kill needlessly.

But early in the sixteenth century, white men, the Spaniards, entered the Colorado Basin. From that time forward, white men had the idea of finding wealth, of taking more than they needed for the moment. Except for the Mormons, they did not come to cultivate the soil or to build homes. They came to take away gold, or buffalo, or beaver—wealth.

29

In a short time the vast herds of bison, which for centuries had blackened the prairie for miles, completely disappeared. Soft-furred beaver would have followed the buffalo to extinction if the fashion from fur to silk hats had not suddenly changed.

A few decades later, herds of cattle and sheep overgrazed the prairies, killing native grasses and making it a desert in many places. The forests faded before the woodsman's ax. Farmers ploughed land that should have remained prairie.

Thus individual greed led to the dust bowls and floods of our own time. More and more people began to see that the land must be conserved, its treasures protected by the federal government for the future.

But let us return to the first of these white invaders, the Spaniards, and their lust for gold.

* * *

These men entered the Colorado Basin from Old Mexico, where they had conquered the Aztecs, an Indian tribe with a high civilization. This conquest is a thrilling story in itself. It began many years before the coming of the Spaniards.

Then the fair god of the Aztecs, Quetzalcoatl, had become angered by the Aztec custom of human sacrifice, so the Indians believed, and had sailed away from the eastern coast, promising some day to return.

At the beginning of the sixteenth century, so many omens

occurred that the superstitious Aztecs believed the time had come for the return of the fair god. Lights had been seen in the eastern heavens. Strange floods and fires had come and gone.

Just then Hernando Cortez, a Spaniard, anchored his ten sailing vessels off the eastern coast of Mexico. The year was 1519.

The news of his arrival was carried quickly by native runner to Montezuma, who reigned at Mexico City. The king half believed that Cortez might be the returned Quetzalcoatl. He sent messengers with gifts of gold, silver, and jewels but warned Cortez not to advance.

But the Spaniards had come to the New World *only* to find gold. "They were afflicted with a disease of the heart, which only gold could cure." They pushed on.

With the aid of rebel subjects of Montezuma, they advanced upon the capital. The simple Indians were greatly frightened by Spanish cannon, spitting thunder and lightning, but even more by horses, snorting and pawing like fabulous beasts. Horses were unknown in the New World. The Indians agreed that these invaders were returned gods.

Montezuma, under a cloud of doubt, did not fight with real conviction. Thus, in a short time the Spaniards conquered the Aztecs and made them slaves.

As year followed year, the Spanish adventurers sent boatload after boatload of precious metals and jewels overseas to fill the strongboxes of the King of Spain.

As the vast wealth of the Aztecs disappeared into the holds of Spanish ships, the Spaniards sought new peoples to exploit, new gold for their coffers. Their appetite was boundless.

31

About this time wanderers brought back to Mexico a story of seven golden cities that lay forty days north in the wilderness. The Spaniards were glad to believe this myth and for many years wandered over the Southwest, driving great herds of cattle, horses, and sheep upon which to live, always searching in vain for the golden cities. Thus herd animals—horses, cattle, sheep—came to America.

These Spaniards endured untold hardship. In their weary migrations they discovered the villages of the Zuni Indians in New Mexico and the Hopi pueblos, which were made neither of gold nor silver but of mud and stone.

Some of these white invaders came upon the Colorado River by land or by sea. Ulloa in 1539 in three sailing vessels reached the mouth of what he thought might be a great river emptying into the Sea of Cortez (Gulf of California), but he turned back without being sure of this.

A year later Alarcón, an ally of Coronado's land force, discovered the mouth of the Colorado and ascended the river some miles but nearly wrecked his boats in the fierce tidal "bore."

The same year, 1540, Cárdenas, a Spanish soldier of Coronado's, stood on the rim and overlooked the Grand Canyon.

But although these soldiers penetrated the wilderness for miles east and northwest, they were not interested in land or river, but in gold. The Colorado was nothing more than a frightful barrier to their mad, fruitless search. After many years, they returned to Mexico, weary, broken in health, and empty-handed.

The land rested almost unmolested until the eighteenth century, when *padres* from Mexico penetrated the wilderness to found missions and convert the Indians to Christianity. These Spanish friars were kindly zealots and often splendid geographers. Such a one was Father Escalante, who crossed the River of the West above Lee's Ferry, called on recent maps "The Crossing of the Fathers," but now hidden under the waters formed by the new Glen Canyon Dam.

The same year, Father Garcés, who visited the Blue Water Indians, made a journey from the mission at Tucson to one on the Pacific coast. He passed on his old gray mule through the region of the Grand Canyon. But some years later, in 1781, this gentle, simple friar was killed by the Yuma Indians in their historic uprising against the Spaniards. The mission work of the fathers on the Colorado River vanished forever. River, Indians, desert, returned to their old solitude.

BEAVER HATS

Twenty years later, beaver hats became fashionable in the cities of the Old and New Worlds. A hat of expensive beaver fur was the only proper headgear for a gentleman.

Beaver were plentiful in the headwaters of the Colorado River. Thus the great fur companies of the time built posts and forts in the Northwest. The age of beaver trappers and mountain men began.

These men were hardy, independent, and fearless, often hunting alone in the mountains an entire season. From the

Indians they learned of trails over the land. They, rather than the scouts and soldiers who followed them, were the first true "trail blazers."

Dressed in buckskin, their uncut hair flowing long over their shoulders, they lived like Indians. Often they married Indian women and lived in buffalo skin lodges. Proudly they called themselves "mountain men."

From the years 1825-35, when beaver trapping was at its height, the mountain men and Indians would gather in some sheltered valley to trade their season's catch of fur. These meetings were called "rendezvous" from a French word meaning a get-together. Such rendezvous were held in Ogden's Hole, Pierre's Hole, Jackson's Hole, Brown's Hole, and Green River Valley.

At an appointed time agreed upon the summer before, merchants from St. Louis unloaded sugar, coffee, traps, guns, powder, whiskey from their mules, setting up a temporary store.

Peaceful, fur-trapping Indians would pitch their buffalo lodges nearby to trade. Lonely trappers would bring in their season's catch. The rendezvous might last several days, or a week or so. Gambling, racing, betting, fighting, and drinking raw whiskey, the trapper, at the end of a wild week often found himself in debt to the traders for his next winter's pelts. But he had a glorious time, his pent-up loneliness bursting forth in wild orgies.

Then, the rendezvous over, the trader loaded his mules or boats with valuable beaver pelts and started back to St. Louis. The trapper looked ahead to a solitary year in the mountains.

A GALLANT TRAPPER

When the beaver days were at their height, William Ashley, of St. Louis, came west, intending to make a quick fortune in beaver. He had hired other young men to trap with him.

When Ashley reached the mountain streams at the head-waters of the Colorado, he found that they were trapped out. He decided to find fresh beaver grounds down Green River, an unknown stream.

At that time there were many stories afloat about this river—stories of rapids, falls, deep canyons. But Ashley was unafraid.

The trappers built three "buffalo" boats of willow frames, covered with green hide. It was spring when they descended the upper Green from Green River Valley. Everything went well for the first few days. They found plenty of game and beaver, and the waters were quiet.

But as they proceeded south the cliffs rose, and they soon encountered furious rapids and dangerous whirlpools. They had to portage around a great fall. Here Ashley painted his name and the date of this voyage on an overhanging rock. In 1869 Major Powell saw Ashley's record. It was seen by later explorers also. Very likely it has now faded away, worn by water and winds.

After fighting with rapids for several weeks and trapping fewer and fewer beaver, Ashley decided it was useless to go on. Besides, his men were frightened at the great gloom and immense depth of the canyons. The boats were abandoned and the trappers returned to the headwaters of the river on foot.

But from William Ashley's inscription on the great rock above Ashley Falls, we know that this gallant trapper from St. Louis was probably the first white man to descend very far into the canyons of Green River, the upper Colorado.

* * *

The romantic, colorful days of the trappers were coming to a close. In the early 1830's, a silk hat was invented to replace the fashionable, expensive fur hat. It was cheap, for it was made by machinery. This spelled the doom of the mountain men. The price of beaver pelt dropped from $6 to $1 a pound. Trappers were no longer willing to endure loneliness, danger, starvation for $1 beaver.

By 1840, a few trappers lived in the mountains. Another few years, and, except for a solitary gold seeker picking at the red cliffs of the Colorado, country and rivers returned again to the red men.

A NEW PROMISED LAND

Then, two years before the Gold Rush, a small band of persecuted people entered the region drained by the River of the West. These were Mormons of the Church of Jesus Christ of Latter-Day Saints.

Some years before, they had been driven from New York to Ohio, and then to Missouri, because of their religion and their custom of plural marriages.

In Missouri and then in Illinois, trouble again arose in the form of persecution and violence and, in 1846, the Saints left for the Far West. Beyond the Rocky Mountains they hoped to find a Promised Land in which to live alone.

Led by Brigham Young, a Moses to his people, the Mormons travelled westward over the Oregon Trail to Green River. Then they turned southwest into the unknown desert of Utah.

As the basin of the Great Salt Lake unfolded before them, Young remembered the Dead Sea of the Hebrews who, too, had fled from persecution to a Land of Promise.

By the shores of another Dead Sea, he would build a new land flowing with milk and honey. "This is the Place," he said to his people, and within an hour the men were ploughing and planting potatoes.

The reclamation of the desert began. The Mormons were the first white men to build homes in the West, to till the soil, and make friends with the Indians.

During the fall and winter of 1847, they suffered greatly, for the first crop was scanty. Emigrants were arriving continually, and there were constantly more mouths to feed. The wheat fields of the following summer promised a splendid harvest. However, out of a clear sky, a great danger threatened to wipe out these people. Down from the mountains swooped a black cloud of Rocky Mountain crickets, millions of them, like a plague of ancient Egypt. Eating everything as they went, they stripped the land bare.

The Mormons were frantic. Death stared them in the face. They fell upon their knees, praying for deliverance. They grabbed sticks, clothing, bags, and met the living flood. They tried to burn the insects, to drown them in the irrigation ditches. It was a battle to the death—insects or farmers.

As the struggle began to seem hopeless, another cloud ap-

proached from the west—a cloud of sea gulls. Had they come to devour the fields too?

But no, the birds fell upon the insects, eating, disgorging, and eating again. After a few days the fields were saved. The Mormons thanked God for delivering them from the plague. Now they were convinced God meant they were to stay in the promised land.

A temple was begun. A city began to grow near the Dead

39

Sea, the Great Salt Lake. Small settlements spread southwest along the streams. They were neat and orderly. The houses were of brick, like New England houses, with steep-pitched roofs, solid and substantial. Picket fences surrounded the gardens. Irrigation ditches followed the roads. Great windbreaks of poplar trees shot their feathery branches skyward. The streets were wide.

The social life of the people was as orderly as their towns. The weak, the poor, the sick were cared for by the group.

As more and more pilgrims came westward each year, Brigham Young began to dream of a great western empire, the "Deseret." But through the middle of the empire flowed the haughty Colorado River.

Then came Young's devoted disciple. Honest Jacob Hamblin knew more than any other Mormon of his day about this strange river. This missionary to the Indians was sent by Young to explore passages across it; to improve trails, to make maps, and to start small settlements.

Jacob has been called the Leatherstocking of Utah. He was a simple, quiet man, content to live and die unknown. He travelled everywhere in the wilderness, studying Indian languages and customs, becoming a friend to them, and always treating them fairly. In a short time he had more influence among them than any other man of his time.

Sometimes guided by the Indians, sometimes alone, God-fearing Jacob Hamblin forded the great Colorado many times in his travels east and west. He knew the crossing at Lee's Ferry, the Crossing of the Fathers, and Pierce's Ferry. He climbed the

Jacob Hamlin

north rim of the Grand Canyon in the hope of discovering some trail across the river to the south rim. Hamblin travelled by boat down the Colorado from Grand Wash, at the end of the Grand Canyon, to the mouth of the Virgin River. Many years later Major Powell used his record on his own famous trip.

Both Jacob and Brigham Young realized that the canyon stream was useless in the region of its chasms. But to the south where the waters slackened the country stretched out. Here the church planned to bring up emigrants and supplies from Fort Yuma to the mouth of the Virgin River. They built Fort Callville and contracted with a boat captain to deliver freight to this fort.

But the boats encountered a great obstacle in the river below Black Canyon—a huge boulder that dammed the stream and made treacherous rapids.

To overcome this, iron rings were imbedded in the cliffs, and tow lines unwound from the drum of a steam winch. Boats were let up or down over the rapids by this method.

But it was soon found that transportation up the Colorado River was too dangerous and costly. After a few trips, Fort Callville was abandoned. Even the practical, energetic Mormons found the River of the West unusable. It could not be tamed.

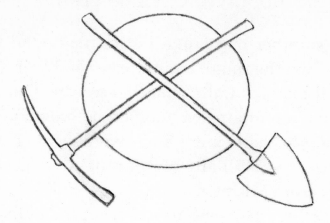

GOLD AGAIN

Two years after the Mormons had settled in Utah, a man discovered Gold in California.

Within a few weeks the news had spread all over the world. A vast migration of peoples started westward—afoot, by boat, on wheels, and on horseback.

Thousands of covered wagon caravans left Omaha and St. Louis converging on the Oregon Trail and following the South Platte to the Rockies where many years before a fur trapper had discovered an easy way over the South Pass.

This pass was so gradual that wagons had no difficulty in crossing it. A Belgian priest of the time claimed the Oregon Trail was one of the finest natural highways in the entire world.

Beyond South Pass, the trail wound down to Green River and then branched, one fork moving northwest to Oregon, the other, the Old Spanish Trail, southwest by Great Salt Lake to California.

BULLWHACKER-BOATMEN

In the late summer of 1849, a California-bound wagon caravan rolled down the rough trail into Green River Valley. It was
too late for it to reach California that season. The snow-capped
Sierra Nevada mountains would soon be snowbound.

Seven bullwhackers, mere boys, were driving the ox teams.
One of these was William Manley of Michigan. The other
youths were from Missouri.

During the long trip over the prairies, the bullwhackers had
heard many stories about the feud between the Mormons and
the Missourians.

Being from that state, they were frightened by these terrifying stories, especially when Manley heard the leader of the
train say that the party would remain over the winter in Salt
Lake City.

Fearful of staying in the city of the dreaded Mormons, Man-
ley recalled the remark of a soldier, some days before, that
Green River flowed into the Colorado, the Colorado into the
Pacific Ocean. Why could they not go to California by boat?
Why not?

Manley told his companions this bit of news, and they decided to leave the wagon caravan at Green River. There were
many *ifs* in their scheme; *if* the river were wide; *if* there were
no rapids; *if* they could find a boat.

When they reached Green River, they found an old ferryboat,
half-covered with sand and mud, and two oars. They dug it out
and, happy over their good luck, bought bacon and flour from

44

the train leader who, no doubt, was glad to be rid of them. Soon they were cheerfully floating downstream in their "Pacific-Ocean-or-Bust" ferryboat, with Manley head of the crew. They were young and gay and adventurous.

The river was quiet. Game was plentiful. The boys felt pleased with themselves. Joking about the stupid, plodding pioneers and their ten miles a day in the dust and heat of the desert, they floated along.

When they met a band of Indians along shore they waved at them gaily, happy not to have met them on the prairie.

When the rapids of Red Canyon began, the mariners tried to fend their awkward, rotten old craft from the rocks with long poles. But the current was strong. It was pinned between two great rocks. They could not budge it. So ended their Pacific-Ocean-or-Bust ferryboat.

But along the shore were pine trees. These suggested dugouts. Working strenuously night and day, the boys soon hacked out four rough canoes and continued the adventure, still cheerful and gay.

But when the canoes entered the rapids of Lodore Canyon laughter stopped. Many times the crude boats upset in the cataracts and whirlpools. All but two guns were sunk in the river. The cliffs were dark and menacing. The youths labored stubbornly on and after many days swept out of Lodore Canyon into the quieter waters below. They had begun to wonder if they would not have been safer in the hands of the Mormons than in the claws of such a terrifying river.

As the boats glided down Desolation Canyon, a gunshot was

heard. Indians were camped along the river. Manley signalled and found them friendly. Their chief was Walker, an historic character, at that time kindly to the white men. He took the youths into his lodge, showing them knives, guns, blankets which he had gotten from the "Mormonee," meaning the Mormons.

The chief asked Manley if he were a "Mormonee."

Manley was quickwitted. He saw that it was safe to be a Mormon. So, placing his hand upon his breast, he said firmly and distinctly, "Mormonee," and the Indians were satisfied.

The boys then asked the Indian chief about the river downstream. Walker led the adventurers to a smooth sandbar. Taking a stick, he drew the Green and Colorado Rivers in the sand with remarkable care and accuracy. Then he gathered rocks, piling them on either side of the drawing to show the canyons as they appeared.

But the farther south he drew the river, the higher became the pile of rocks. Finally Walker had not enough rocks to show the great depths of the canyons. By signs and grunts he described death by drowning or by savage Indians who might await the voyagers down the river.

The mariners were now thoroughly discouraged and frightened. They decided the Mormons might be kinder to them than the River of the West. The following day, Walker gave Manley and four of his companions several pack horses. With careful directions from the Indian they finally reached the California Trail. Two boys remained with Walker, but later they, too, after many hardships, reached the settlements.

The gaiety and light-heartedness with which Manley and his friends battled the most dangerous river in the world makes it the most intriguing among early known canyon voyages.

A SOLDIER TRIES

From where the Oregon Trail crossed the upper Colorado at Green River Valley, for many hundreds of miles south, the River of Mystery is protected by great cliffs, impossible to traverse.

But less than a hundred miles from the Gulf of California the river listlessly meanders, quietly and peacefully. Here crossed the Gila River Trail from Santa Fe. On this desert trail for years trod *padres*, trappers, emigrants to the Pacific Coast.

With the rush of gold-seekers and emigrants to southern California, forts were built along this trail to protect pioneers from the fury of the Apache Indians.

About 1858 an official in the War Department in Washington studied the map and wondered why the harmless-looking Colorado would not carry supplies from its mouth to Fort Yuma, possibly even farther north. Captain Ives of the United States Army was sent west to find out more about this strange river.

A boat, the *Explorer*, was built for him in sections and shipped to the Gulf of California, where it was assembled.

Ives began the perilous journey up the river. At that season, the tidal bore was very high and very furious. The *Explorer* was not built to escape sand bars, snags, hidden rocks so typical of the muddy stream. But the courageous Ives continued, fighting many hardships, until in Black Canyon, present site of Hoover Dam, his vessel hit a rock and was disabled.

Thus Captain Ives found, as had the Spaniards, the trappers, the Mormons, and all men who came before, that this great, fierce river of the west was useless to man. Ives reported to the government: "It seems that, by Nature, the Colorado River, along the greater portion of its lonely and majestic way, shall be forever unvisited and undisturbed."

But only ten years later came the man who dared to question him—Major John Wesley Powell.

4. Powell, the Man Who Dared

Three years after the Civil War had ended between the States, a black-bearded, sturdy man, John Wesley Powell, stood on the brink of Green River. His right sleeve hung empty, for he had left an arm on the battlefield of the late war.

Major Powell was a geologist as well as a soldier. For several summers he had explored along the headwaters of the Colorado River of the West. Slowly the lure of these lonely desert streams had grown upon him.

Where did the Green and Grand Rivers, as they were then called, give birth to the unknown river, the River of Mystery? No one knew, for no white man had ever seen this birth.

As Major Powell brooded thoughtfully on the rim of Lodore Canyon, an idea that had been slowly growing within him came to life. He resolved to explore by boat the chasms of the Colorado. He must know if the weird stories told by Indians, trappers, and prospectors, of underground caverns and great falls were really true.

Powell had the yearning of the true explorer. He was willing to risk his life to learn the truth about the River of Mystery. He was a strong-willed, unbending, and as stubborn as a bulldog.

A year later, in the spring of 1869, a Union Pacific train stopped at a little frontier station on Green River in Wyoming. The railroad had just been finished.

Major Powell descended with nine men. They carried four well-built river boats to the bank of the stream. Major Powell's great adventure was begun.

The four sturdy boats were packed with supplies—ropes, tools, scientific instruments, but no life preservers. Into water-tight compartments, fore and aft, went food to last for ten months.

Powell did not know how long the conquest of the river would take. The water might freeze over in the winter. Then he would be compelled to wait for the ice to melt. At that time, no one knew that the swift current of the Colorado rarely freezes.

The onlookers who had come down from the frontier settlement to see the start of this exploration must have thought the one-armed Powell mad indeed. No man had ever gone down the river and come back alive.

On the 24th of May the heavily-loaded boats slid into the quiet waters of upper Green River, and the Powell expedition was off.

For five hundred miles the Green flows south until it joins the Grand. In these five hundred miles the explorers soon learned the varied dangers of this stream which were only a prelude to the greater dangers on the Colorado.

Sharp rocks lay unseen beneath the muddy waters, eager to tear holes in the boats. Whirlpools could suck down even the most powerful of swimmers. In Lodore Canyon, the rapids were almost continuous.

For days and days the men dragged their water-soaked boats

Major Powell

around cataracts too dangerous to run, spraining backs, mashing toes and fingers. The nights at that altitude were cold, even under blankets. Sometimes the wreck of an ancient boat or half-buried tools of a drowned miner warned them of their own possible future.

In the rapids of Lodore Canyon one boat hit a rock, breaking into a thousand pieces. Food and instruments were lost in the river. The three passengers in the little craft swam to a rocky island and were rescued. In their fright they laid the blame for the accident on Powell. Friction began to grow between the men in the party, frightened as they were.

Later a small accident might have become a serious one when a spark from the camp fire turned the dry willows along the shore into a blazing furnace. The men saved themselves by running to their boats.

In Labyrinth and Desolation Canyons the mariners felt the weariness of the winding river, bending in great oxbows, but never seeming to get anywhere.

Dust storms harried the waters. Dead camp fires, tepee poles warned them of wandering Indians. In the alarming gloom cast at twilight by the high cliffs, any danger seemed possible.

Two months passed. In the middle of July, the bronzed, hardened men finally reached the junction of the two great tributaries, the Green and the then-named Grand, and the river they had been seeking began—the Colorado.

No white man had ever before stood on this miserable, arid spot. There was no map, record, or chart of what lay downstream between rapidly rising walls.

The explorers camped at the junction for several days calking their battered boats with piñon gum, making scientific observations, and screening lumps out of their damp flour. Of the ten months' food they had started with, only enough to last two months remained. Yet the men had hardly begun their great adventure. Food had to be rationed daily.

Many a night Powell lay sleepless, rolled up in his blanket, wondering about the future. Would he reach a spot where the river rushed over an impassable fall, between vertical cliffs, where they could not climb up, go on, or return?

Meanwhile, in the outside world, the newspapers were spreading a weird story of the collapse of the Powell expedition. An eastbound passenger on the train from Green River told other passengers that he had stood at Brown's Hole and had seen, with his own eyes, Major Powell and his companions swallowed up by a whirlpool. Many people believed this tale.

But the voyagers were just beginning their battle with Cataract Canyon, formed by the marriage of the two great tributaries. The dangers of this forty-mile chasm were almost as great as those of the Grand Canyon itself.

The explorers did not know how long the furious rapids would continue. For days they wearily portaged over the rocks, around cataracts, marvelling at the cliffs that now rose over two thousand feet into the sky. In the gloomy abyss, they tried to keep up their courage by songs and jokes, but Powell writes that their jests were hollow, and under their laughter each man feared the next hour and the next day.

Then a week later, to their infinite relief, the cliffs broke down into pinnacles, the waters quietened, and the terrors of Cataract Canyon became like the memory of a bad dream.

The tired, hungry men were little prepared for the beauties of Glen Canyon that followed. For over one hundred and fifty miles the Colorado flowed between low, red walls, riddled with ancient cliff dwellings of the red men. Never again would the river be as peaceful or as charming as in this canyon. There were no dust storms, no rapids, no whirlpools. The green glens, the charming grottoes tempted them to rest.

There were arrowheads to collect, ruined cliff dwellings to explore, soft rocks in which to cut their names. But as these men floated on mile after mile, they expected at each turn of the gentle river to hear the boom of rapids that never came.

After a week of calm and peace, a small stream came in from the west, the Paria, and the character of the river changed. The soft red rocks of Glen Canyon that meant quiet water were replaced by hard, black, glossy limestone, a kind of marble. The cliffs rose; the water roared. Downstream lay Marble Canyon, the beginning of Grand Canyon, the longest, hardest, most dangerous stretch of river in the world, almost three hundred miles of rapids, whirlpools, and mile-high cliffs.

Food was vanishing; there was still coffee, some flour, dried apples, but the bacon had spoiled and was thrown away. Hurrying on before starvation would catch up with them, the explorers entered Marble Canyon.

The river bellowed like a mad bull. The men could not hear

each other speak. It rained almost daily. The river might rise suddenly and overwhelm them during the night, for this was the season of furious cloudbursts on the desert.

One wet night, the men sat on a narrow ledge above the booming river, trying to sleep sitting up, for the shelf was too narrow for them all to lie down. The black marble walls added to their gloom. The bodily fear was great, but the spiritual fear was greater. Many men, in the depths of these gorges, have felt they were slowly going mad. Some mariners have lost their power to walk and have crawled, white and shaken, over the rocks.

In such gloom, the Powell party reached the mouth of the little Colorado River and entered the Granite Gorge, the very heart of the Grand Canyon.

Even sturdy, manly Powell felt he was losing his mind. The friction between the men had increased since the first boat was lost in Lodore Canyon. They were hungry; they were nervous. No one knew how long the "white hell" would last, for the barometers were useless.

On they struggled, and at last, on the 21st of August, the hated black granite gave way to soft red sandstone. The cliffs lowered. The rapids lessened. The nerves and fears of the men grew less tense. Each one hoped in his heart that the black granite was at an end, that open country would soon begin.

They reached an Indian garden along the river, ripe with squash. They stole all they could carry and downstream had a feast of green food. Their spirits were lighter than they had been in days. They felt that the end was in sight.

And then, without any warning, like the boom of cannon,

the feared black granite closed in upon them again. Each man recoiled in horror. More rapids, more hunger, more danger! Only musty flour remained and coffee. Ten days' supply of food lay in the boats.

They reached Separation Rapids. There terrifying cascades boomed, roared, menaced! Was this the place Powell had envisioned in his long and sleepless nights?

The Major studied Separation Rapids all afternoon. Somehow they had to be run. There was no other way but on, on, on.

The leader called his men together. He told them in the morning they must pilot the boats through the boiling waters. Like a bomb the friction that had been growing for months violently burst. Three of the men refused to go on. They would climb the cliffs and take their chances with the Indians. Their nerves were frayed to ribbons.

Powell argued with them, trying to convince them that the canyon was almost at an end. He sat up all of the night trying to plot his course without the aid of a barometer. He figured it was not more than ninety miles to the mouth of the Virgin River. Up the Virgin he knew was help.

During the night Powell himself weakened. But when he thought of the years he had planned this trip, he could not leave the job so nearly finished.

In the morning, the three men were still determined. They took guns but refused food and began the hard climb to the rim above the river.

Now only two boats were needed. Powell led the first one through Separation Rapids safely. The other one followed him, also safely. They were so discouraged the day before that perhaps they had exaggerated the danger of the rapids.

For several hours the Major and his men waited downstream below Separation Rapids, hoping the dissenters who had gone would change their minds and follow. When they did not appear, the party went on.

Two days later Powell and his men reached the end of the Grand Canyon. From here on, the record of the Mormon missionary Jacob Hamblin guided them to the mouth of the Virgin River.

What became of the three deserters? They reached the rim above the river after a hard climb and met the Shewits Indians, who were friendly at first and took them into their camp. They told the Indians they had come down the Colorado. This the Indians could not believe.

During the night, members of the tribe came in from the north, reporting outrages on Indians by white miners. The Shewits believed their guests were guilty and had not come down the river. In the morning, as the white men returned from a water hole, the Indians ambushed and killed them.

Meanwhile Powell had reached the mouth of the Virgin River. Three Mormons were on the river, watching for wreckage of his party, as news had come from Salt Lake to look out for broken boats. They were more surprised at seeing the Major alive than he was at seeing them.

Thus ended the first conquest of the Colorado River. Now it was no longer the River of Mystery. Powell had solved the riddle.

As the years passed, other adventurers followed in Powell's footsteps—Galloway, Loper, the Brown-Stanton party, Stone, the Kolb brothers, the Geographic Society, and others. These also were brave men, but some of them were aided in their exploration by modern inventions like the radio, by a more settled country, and by food hidden in places along the river. Powell had none of these aids, and his is still the great glory of uncovering the secret of the unknown Colorado River.

5. The Runaway River

In the very southeastern part of California, there once lay a sandy lifeless desert. Today it is a green valley, the Imperial Valley, where fruits and vegetables ripen early for the tables of the world.

The Colorado River is the kindly wizard whose magic wand changed this desert into a garden. This story begins many thousands of years ago.

Then, the Gulf of California sprawled more than a hundred miles north of its present boundary. Its ancient coast line is clear, even today, at the feet of the Santa Rosa Mountains where sea shells are still found.

At that time the muddy Colorado River to the east emptied midway into this long arm of the sea. Daily it deposited a heavy load of silt which it pushed farther and farther out into the salty blue waters of the Gulf.

As the years passed, the mound grew longer, until it crossed the gulf to its western shore. The upper part then became a lake, with no outlet to the sea, for the changeable river, in some spring flood, had carved a new channel to the ocean, passing by the lake it had once made.

Slowly the waters in the lake dried up, leaving only a shallow, sandy basin below sea level, blistering in the hot sun.

61

Then, perhaps a thousand years or more later, the erratic Colorado once more cut its way back into the desert basin, slowly filling it with water. When it became full it may have overflowed south into the ocean again—no one knows. But we do know that the river once more changed its course and the lake dried up again and became a desert.

This constant change from lake to desert, desert to lake, occurred many times during the centuries. The fitful Colorado was like the pendulum of a liquid clock. It swung westward, and the desert became a lake. It swung eastward, and the lake changed to a desert.

The river was never certain of its course through the sandy delta to the sea. In flood time it made and unmade a course, carving one out, then filling it again.

In the early part of the sixteenth century, the Spaniards, in their weary, fruitless search for the Seven Cities of Cibola, came upon the basin, then a desert.

It was still a desert when the Forty-niners crossed its deadly wastes on their way to the Pacific. Then it was called the Salton Sink, meaning a salty hole.

One of these gold-seekers was a Doctor Wolzencraft. He observed how close to the sink flowed the great western river. He studied the ancient overflow channels which the Colorado had once dug into the basin, and the idea came to him that through these channels water might be used to irrigate the wasteland of sandy desert.

Dr. Wolzencraft was full of enthusiasm for this plan. He preached the gospel of reclaiming the desert everywhere he went. But at the time it was not fully realized, as it is now, that irrigated desert lands will produce bountiful crops. People only laughed at the harmless dreamer.

As the years passed and the nineteenth century came to a close, the reclamation of desert lands succeeded in other parts of the world. Men began to look upon the Salton Sink with new eyes.

But it was not until 1900 that a company was launched to reclaim the Sink, renamed then the Imperial Valley. A year later the California Development Company dug a canal from the Colorado River near Yuma, connecting it to the old Alamo, an overflow channel that the river had onced carved into the valley in ancient times.

The land was opened to settlers, and in a short time Dr. Wolzencraft's vision of green fields began to be realized as thousands of acres were plowed and seeded.

The blinding yellow sands gave way to fields of alfalfa; sickly sagebrush disappeared, replaced by orchards of oranges, dates, figs, lemons.

The growing season was twelve months long; there were no frosts. In only a few years the once-desert became a great forcing house—a hot house whose products were the first to reach the eastern market.

As the richness of the basin became widely known, thousands of new settlers poured in. By 1904, ten thousand farmers needed water for their countless fields.

But the water was decreasing! The long, winding Alamo river that brought water from the Colorado lay forty-five of its

fifty miles in Old Mexico. It was silting up. Four miles of canal near the entrance were so choked with silt that water could not flow freely to the withering fields.

Law suits began to rain down upon the heads of the water company officials. But they were helpless, for they were bankrupt. To dredge out the channel would have cost money they did not have.

Something must be done and done quickly! Without careful thought of what it might mean, the engineers of the California Development Company made a fifty-foot cut in the west bank of the Colorado River, south of the international line.

A short canal was dug from this breach to the Alamo canal, joining it below the silted-up section. Water once more flowed to the fields and orchards.

If the engineers had known what an unusual flood season was about to occur on the Colorado they would have strengthened the bank of the stream instead of cutting into it.

During the winter of 1904-1905 one flood after another came rushing down the Colorado, each one widening the crevasse the engineers had made.

In the spring of 1905 it was at last decided to close the cut, and then the greatest of all floods pounded down the Colorado, tearing out sandbags, brush, and earth fill placed in its way. Soon the entire river began to pour into Imperial Valley in a great brown torrent, settling in the lowest part and forming a new Salton Sea.

Time and time again the river crushed each attempt man made to control it. The farmers became worried. Their fields were dying. The tracks of the Southern Pacific Railroad into the valley were under water.

In this emergency, the railroad took over the affairs of the bankrupt California Development Company and by August 1905 began a series of battles with the runaway river.

Many prominent engineers visited Imperial Valley during that summer. But no two of them could agree upon what to do. Never before in history had men tried to control such a great stream of water, rushing down a steep slope of sandy soil into a basin below sea level large enough to hold Long Island Sound. Most of the engineers believed there was only a fighting chance of saving Imperial Valley.

By the fall of 1905 the entire river flowed into the basin, and the Salton Sea rose seven inches every day. Fields were so furrowed with chasms they were abandoned. Towns were partly destroyed.

Time and time again mattresses of brush and cable were woven and laid down in the breach which had now increased to over a thousand feet. But each time the raging river brushed them lightly away, as a giant would brush off a fly.

Could a rock fill be used? Some engineers believed the rock would sink into the sandy river bottom and disappear. But rock was tried and did not sink.

So, after the fourth failure to harness the river, it was decided to dump rock into the breach faster than the river could carry it downstream. This was the last chance left; everything else had failed.

Rock quarries lay several hundred miles east in Arizona and

farther north in California. These quarries were opened. Soon great trainloads of rock began to chug up over mountain passes.

Terminals were built to the crevasse, thousands of side cars were borrowed for dumping rock. Ten complete work trains were assembled. Masses of equipment were purchased—pile drivers, steam shovels, wire, cable, timber, horses, mules.

In a country where the temperature may zoom from sixty degrees at night to one hundred and twenty-five in the day, the problem of labor was serious. Few white men could stand the heat of the delta lands.

Indians, used to the climate, were hired. These Indians and their families came—the Cocopas, Pimas, Papagos, Yumas. Martial law was imposed, for the great battle took place in Mexico.

Then the first offensive began. Trestles were built over the cut; mattresses of brush, wire, and cable were woven. The bottom of the stream was blanketed with these. Up over the trestles puffed great locomotives, pulling side cars loaded with rock. Red-turbaned Indians pushed the rock off into the swirling brown waters below. The rocks too large to handle were broken down with shots of dynamite.

Day after day, night after night, the battle went on.

The brush mattresses held the weight of the rock. The pile grew higher. Just as the tide of battle turned to the side of the engineers, a bypass that carried part of the river gave way, carrying down to the Salton Sea a two hundred foot headgate. Barred in one place, the Colorado burst out in another. The labor of weeks disappeared in an hour.

This ended the fifth attempt to stop the runaway river. One

ray of hope remained. The rock barrier did hold. If rock could be dumped even faster, the engineers believed they might everlastingly win over the river.

For the sixth time the fight started over again. Day after day, night after night, for weeks the mad dumping of rock into the aroused, angry river went on. In three weeks the battle was over. The Colorado was forced into its old channel, and flowed sullenly to the ocean. The engineers had won.

But the celebration over the victory had hardly died away when a great flood came down the Gila River, tributary of the Colorado near Yuma.

The river was in a surly mood. It was hard hit but not beaten. It searched for a weak place in the earthen levee and found it, just south of where the breach had been closed.

It dug a hole, very small at first, and unseen. The hole grew larger. At midnight, on the 7th of December, 1906, the bank caved in. Soon, through a breach that grew to a thousand feet in a few days, the entire Colorado River triumphantly poured into the Salton Sea.

Would the river *never* be conquered? Would Imperial Valley again, as in times past, become a lake?

The engineers said "No." Back came the red-turbaned Indians and their families; back came horses, mules, pile drivers, and great trainloads of rock.

For an entire month men and machinery labored to erect a trestle that would stand. The river ripped out three before the engineers conquered.

There was no time to weave brush mattresses. Rock must be

68

dumped at once. Again the groaning trains puffed up. Once more the Indians dumped rock, day and night, into the bitter and angry Colorado.

The new year came and went. At last on the 10th of January, 1907, over two years after the first cut was made, the mighty Colorado faltered. Slowly, foot by foot, man forced it back into its ancient channel, to flow harmlessly to the sea. The fields were saved!

Even though the defenses raised by the engineers in their struggle stood firm, the threat of flood, imagined or real, hung constantly over Imperial Valley like a sword about to fall.

Millions of dollars were spent in reinforcing the levees up and down the river. Floods came in 1909, 1911, and in 1916—not disasters like the one of 1904 but severe enough to increase the fear of the farmers.

In the meantime, the wealth of the valley had grown. For a quarter of a century men argued and argued; what could be done? As the years passed, it became clear that only a dam built upstream in the regions of the canyons, would finally control the unpredictable Colorado.

Thus it came about, twenty-five years after the runaway river had made the Salton Sea, that Hoover Dam was planned and built.

6. The Giant Chained

Water is the most precious thing in the Plateau land, where rain so rarely falls. Each western state through which the Colorado River flowed had rights to its water.

As the years passed and a dam to control the wild stream became necessary, these states quarreled over water, just as children quarrel over money willed by their dead father. The conflict became so serious that at one time people thought the states could never agree.

But Herbert Hoover, in 1922, settled the disputes, and each state signed the Colorado River Compact.

The dam was assured!

Where should it be built?

For over thirty years, the Reclamation Service of the Government had geologists and engineers in the field to map the Colorado River, for Uncle Sam knew that some time the Canyon River of the West must be tamed. There could never again be another Imperial Valley tragedy.

These pioneers of science lived in a desert land without any comfort, without roads or shade, risking their lives on sheer cliffs to place their stakes and flying by plane over the Plateau country to make aerial maps.

They found nineteen possible dam sites along the river. Which one was the best?

About two hundred and fifty miles below the Grand Canyon, almost five hundred miles above the mouth of the river, the Colorado cuts through a narrow box canyon. Cliffs as tough as cast iron tower a thousand feet on both sides of the stream.

Although these rocky walls are of volcanic "breccia," they are less cracked than other cliffs along the Colorado. Yet geologists claim volcanic action stopped thousands of years ago in this spot, Black Canyon.

Solidly welded rocks are essential to make a safe dam. Above Black Canyon the country widens. A natural storage basin stretches over a hundred miles upstream. This basin would hold two entire years' flow of the river; it would give every person on earth five thousand gallons of water. It was an ideal reservoir.

Nearby were found fine deposits of sand and gravel for making concrete out of which the great obstruction could be built.

Several hundred miles southwest were the growing, ever-thirsty cities of Southern California, eager for water and power. In fifty years these cities would pay Uncle Sam back for his investment in the dam by buying power from him.

The engineers of the Reclamation Service believed Black Canyon was the best site on the river and began plans.

The dam would be the highest ever made, seven hundred and twenty-seven feet high. It must be very strong, as strong as modern engineers could make it. It must never break.

Downstream lay fertile Imperial Valley, and the dam was chiefly built to protect this green, under-sea-level basin. So the plans were conservative, leaning far on the side of safety.

Almost ten years after the seven western states signed the

Colorado River Compact, the contract was let to Six Companies of San Francisco to build the dam. It was allowed seven years and $54,000,000 with which to do it.

A land without trees or life, so dry that even the Indians shunned it, suddenly teemed with men.

In the pit of Black Canyon, before a road was built to the river, drills began to bite into the rocks on either side of the stream. A thousand men constructed four tunnels which, when finished, would carry the Colorado River around the dam site.

Then, in the dry river bed, the foundation could be laid.

From the rim of the abyss, "scalers" hung by ropes, cleaning the cliffs of loose rock so that no workman below might be killed by falling boulders. This was a dangerous job, something that the excitement-loving Apache Indians enjoyed most of all.

On these same lifeless cliffs went up giant steel derricks to support the aerial cableways that would carry men and machines, in the flick of an eyelash, any place on the mammoth job.

Six miles away on the desert, the government was busy constructing a planned modern city for the workmen—a city to house five thousand people, with paved streets, gardens, mess halls, and dormitories, some of which would be air-cooled. It was named Boulder City.

The climate of Nevada and Arizona varies greatly, from twenty to one hundred and thirty degrees at times. If white men were to build Boulder Dam, the government knew they could do so only if they had good living conditions.

Close by a factory was erected to roll and weld steel pipes for

Original site of Hoover Dam

the thirty-foot penstock tunnels. These pipes were too large to be made elsewhere and carried overland by train, so they were made on the spot.

Railroads had to be built, highways from Las Vegas laid out, and cement plants constructed.

A little over a year after the job had started, two tunnels were finished on the Arizona side of the river, and the Colorado River flowed through them. Then steam shovels wormed their way down far below the old water line into the solid rock, and the foundation of the dam was begun.

Every day in the pitiless summers, when the rocks were so hot they burned a gloveless hand, every day in winter when the cold winds blew up and down the canyon, men worked without stopping. Even in the night the mysterious canyon, lit up by great lamps, was as bright as midday, and the work continued around the clock. Even on Sundays and holidays drills bit into the rock, steam shovels whistled, cableways groaned.

Two years passed, and a strange-looking building slowly loomed up from the black pit—a building made of interlocking columns, like huge boxes which a giant might pile carelessly one upon another. A view from the rim revealed how these columns were constructed.

A hook swooped down from a cableway overhead; it grabbed a barrel from a trainload of barrels waiting along the Nevada cliffs; it rose in the air, screeched its way over the yawning abyss, then, quivering, it gently descended until it swayed above a partly finished column.

Men, small as ants, pressed their bodies against the walls of

the form as the bottom of the barrel opened and a pile of gray concrete fell out. The empty barrel rose to the blue sky.

The waiting, booted workmen attacked the mound with tools, spreading it out smoothly to the walls of the column. In another two minutes, a similar barrel dumped sixteen more tons of concrete, and the column grew visibly higher.

Why was the dam built in interlocking columns and not in one solid piece?

This barrier to the Colorado River, Hoover Dam, was the greatest mountain of concrete ever poured at one time—six hundred and fifty feet through at the base—at long as a city block.

When concrete is poured it begins at once to harden, and as it sets it becomes hot. Then, as it slowly cools, cracks often develop through it. The dam was so thick that it would have taken over one hundred and twenty-five years to cool it through naturally.

The engineers could not wait one hundred and twenty-five years to see if the dam would crack. So they hastened the cooling by doing three things, some of them quite new.

They used a special cement that set without getting very hot; they planned cracks between each column for the cement to expand and contract; and then, most interesting of all, they laid miles of pipes through the concrete and in these pipes ran icy cool water. The cold water cooled the concrete soon after it was poured.

When the concrete was cool, the man-made slots, or cracks, and pipes were filled with liquid cement, forced in under great pressure. Thus the dam was a solid mass. Now the engineers were sure no cracks would endanger the dam.

LAKE MEAD

As the concrete walls grew higher, the time came, in 1935, when they could hold back the river, and the diversion tunnels, through which the stream had been flowing for several years, were plugged. Then Lake Mead began to form against the upstream face of Hoover Dam.

As the Colorado River slowed down at the barrier, it dropped three hundred tons of silt a minute to the bottom of the lake. It carries more mud than any other river of America.

Would this silt fill Lake Mead? Experts say it would take at least two centuries, probably more, and in that long time other dams will be built at the many dam sites available. This silt problem later led to the building of Glen Canyon Dam, finished in 1963.

POWER

Meanwhile, from each cliff on the upstream side sprouted four tall intake towers. They are like great sieves. The water enters through them into pressure tunnels that lead into the power houses, and turbines, to make electrical energy.

The power houses were built on the downside face of the structure. Nineteen stories tall, they are completely dwarfed by the great height of the dam. Yet they can house seventeen

great generators, if customers can be found in the Southwest to buy power made by so many generators. At its maximum, Boulder Dam can generate more energy than Niagara Falls, Muscle Shoals, and the Russian dam Dnieprostroy together.

So much energy can be created because Lake Mead is so high. When full it is almost six hundred feet deep. It only takes seven and one-half gallons of water falling less than nine feet each second to make one horsepower.

In the fall of 1935, President Franklin D. Roosevelt dedicated Hoover Dam. A year later a generator hummed in the power house, and power was flowing over a transmission line to light the streets of Los Angeles almost two years ahead of schedule.

OTHER PROJECTS

Three other projects linked to Hoover Dam lie downstream— Parker Dam, the aqueduct to California cities, and the All-American Canal.

One hundred and fifty miles below Black Canyon, Parker Dam was built. Here begins the aqueduct to Los Angeles and surrounding cities, financed by these cities. A billion gallons of water are sucked up daily, purified, and carried in a giant pipe over the desert and through the mountains.

Farther south, in the sandy delta close to the mouth of the great river, a new man-made ditch carries water to the fields of Imperial Valley. This is the All-American Canal, lying only in American territory, that replaces the Alamo canal, used since irrigation began in the valley.

The new canal is so deep and wide it will deliver twenty-five times more water to the fields than the winding old Alamo river.

The building of this mammoth ditch is another conquest over

natural obstacles. For ten miles it burrows through sand hills as stark, as lifeless, as the Sahara Desert. The wind blows and shifts great dunes here and there. These dunes would choke the canal if vegetation were not planted on either side and parts of the ditch lined with rock and concrete.

East of the Colorado, in Arizona, half a million new acres of desert will be irrigated by the river.

* * *

Such vast undertakings as these require millions of dollars to build. Into these projects have gone $165,000,000, of which $70,000,000 constructed Hoover Dam and Lake Mead.

But facts and figures vanish as one overlooks Hoover Dam and reflects how it has changed the heart of the strange river of the West.

From the days of the cliff dwellers, men have feared this giant. Indians, Spaniards, trappers, pioneers hated but secretly admired it.

When Powell set out to solve its mystery, he knew it would be only a matter of luck if he returned alive.

For hundreds of years the Colorado has gone its lonely but glorious way, a river of death. Now man, his science and machines, have chained the giant. Peoples have united peacefully to build a great structure, a symbol of the new age.

From an enemy, the river has become a friend, lifting fear from the farmer, lighting and warming cities, turning wheels, and, above all, bringing life into waste places where no life was.

81

7. Glen Canyon and Lake Powell

Although Hoover Dam chained the fury of the Colorado River forever, engineers worry constantly about the accumulation of silt dropped into Lake Mead daily—three hundred tons every minute. It has been estimated that in a few hundred years Lake Mead would be no longer a lake, but a huge sand pile. Something must be done to stop the silting, but where?

For years this problem puzzled the engineers. At last, in 1963, it was decided a dam must be built upstream. Then the life of Lake Mead might be extended perhaps one hundred and fifty more years.

The site chosen for the new dam lay at the end of that peaceful section of the river loved by trappers, miners, fishermen, explorers alike—Glen Canyon. Here the canyon walls were adequate to anchor a dam. Water behind a dam would spread far, far back among the canyons along the river for almost one hundred or even two hundred miles.

A city, much like Boulder City near Hoover Dam, was built on the bluff above the dam site for the workers and their families.

The Glen Canyon dam, as it was named, was begun and finished in seven years. It was altogether fitting that the great lake formed behind the dam should be called Lake Powell, after the first man to run the "white water" canyons of the Colorado. And so it was named.

Was there ever a lake like Lake Powell? One wonders. Now that the water is stilled and blue, it creeps silently between

great red rocks, handsome buttresses, castle-like formations, natural bridges carved by nature. It fills secret grottos sweet with ferns where animals lived. It covers ancient cliff dwellings. It is indeed the "Land of Standing Rocks," as the Indians called it. Much of the lower part of the lake reminds one of similar places in ancient Egypt as the quiet blue waters reflect the rocks eroded by nature, not man.

There are but few places where the lake widens out. Most of it seems to spread its peaceful path between huge buttes, vast red domes and carved pinnacles of various designs. The impression as the boat glides along is of great labyrinths, secret and mysterious; of a strange, dry, antique world reflected in blue, life-giving water but almost devoid of trees or shrubs. Water in the desert.

Part of the shores of Lake Powell lie in the Navajo Reservation. Here the Navajo Indians protect it, acting as guides, caretakers, and rangers.

Lake Powell is becoming one of the nation's finest playgrounds, teeming with fish, and large enough to have countless silent and secret places to explore and forget the world.

In a practical sense, its huge dynamos will supply needed electricity for the fast-growing upper Colorado River states, Utah, Arizona, New Mexico.

As for the future of the Colorado River, no one can say how far man must go to secure more water for the ever-growing cities of the Southwest. Will he tap the Snake River to the north to add to the water of the Colorado? Will the dreams of the engineers some day come true to tap the Yukon River in the far north or even the great Columbia, pouring its waters into the sea? All of this lies in the future. All this is possible.

But one wonders if the future may not lie in the experiments of desalting seawater, reducing its cost to compete with power from coal, oil, and gas. Will the further development of atomic energy give up cheap and efficient power to lift desalted water anywhere?

Will the time come when the waters of the Colorado, the Snake, the Feather River, even the Yukon, may not be as necessary as they now seem to us?

It could happen that the Colorado River will lapse into its ancient ways. It may be it will no longer be our main source of life. No one knows.

But the great river and gay young stream, as it rises in Colorado and Wyoming and in a few hundred miles becomes one of the wonders of the world, will still be there. Countless thousands of people will still stand on the rim of the Grand Canyon and wonder how Nature, with only water, sand, the slow elevation of the land, but most of all "countless millions of years," has created this greatest of the world's wonders. So the canyons will still be there for man to marvel at.

*   *   *

This is the story of the Colorado River over the centuries. Still the most dangerous, most violent, most moody of any of our rivers and the most majestic, it is also one of our greatest natural treasures, which now makes the sandy wastes of the Southwest bloom richly with life and beauty where only desert once was.

86

The river in repose

Great
Salt Lake
Salt Lake City

N E V A D A

U T A H

Lake
Tahoe   Carson City

Sacramento

BRYCE CANYON
NATIONAL PARK

ZION
NATIONAL PARK

Lake Powell

Virgin R.

GLEN CANYON
DAM   Page

S I E R R A

GRAND
CANYON
NAT. MON.

KAIBAB
FOREST

MARBLE
CANYON

Lake
Mead

Las Vegas

PAINTED
DESERT

N E V A D A

Boulder
City

HOOVER
DAM
(BOULDER DAM)

GRAND CANYON
NATIONAL PARK

Little

R A N G E

C A L I F O R N I A

Verde R.

Havasu
Lake

PARKER
DAM

Los Angeles

Colorado

R.

Aqueduct

River

Salt   R.

Salton Sea

Phoenix

P A C I F I C

River

IMPERIAL VALLEY

IMPERIAL
DAM

San Diego

Gila

River

Yuma

A R I Z O N A

Colorado

O C E A N

Tucson

B A J A

C A L I F.

Gulf of
California

Rolfe

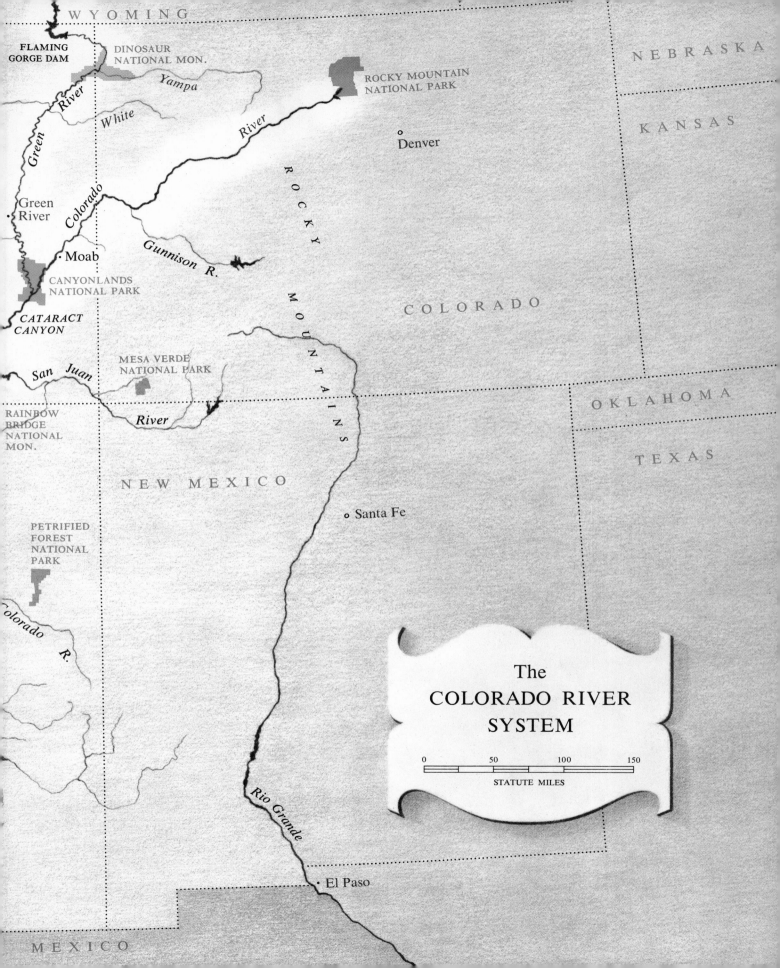

WYOMING

FLAMING
GORGE DAM

DINOSAUR
NATIONAL MON.

Yampa

White

River

ROCKY MOUNTAIN
NATIONAL PARK

Green River

o Denver

Green
River

Colorado

• Moab

Gunnison R.

CANYONLANDS
NATIONAL PARK

*CATARACT
CANYON*

R
O
C
K
Y

M
O
U
N
T
A
I
N
S

C O L O R A D O

NEBRASKA

KANSAS

San Juan

MESA VERDE
NATIONAL PARK

River

RAINBOW
BRIDGE
NATIONAL
MON.

N E W   M E X I C O

OKLAHOMA

TEXAS

PETRIFIED
FOREST
NATIONAL
PARK

o Santa Fe

olorado R.

Rio Grande

• El Paso

The
**COLORADO RIVER
SYSTEM**

0   50   100   150
STATUTE MILES

M E X I C O